Reaching the shore of Surrender

Jan Griffin

Dedication

I dedicate this book to my amazing husband, Greg. You have loved me so deeply, intentionally, and unconditionally! Thank you for your time and energy to help me with this book!

Acknowledgments

I would like to acknowledge the wonderful editing skills of my daughter, Natalie. Even with so much uncertainty in your life over the past several months, you did it and loved doing it. Thank you also to my son, Matt, and his wife, Alana, and my daughter, Heidi, for their love and support throughout my imperfect parenting. Thank you to Dee and Aunt Rosie for your support and belief in me and this book. Finally, I want to thank Sarah Brooks, my writing coach, who provided wonderful guidance and advice and encouraged me to consider self-publishing.

Table of Contents

No Footprints in the Sand

It was a sunny, warm spring day on the golden beach in Florida, close to where we lived. At age 8, the salty smell of the ocean and the gentle sun-filled breeze poured around me like heavenly waves crashing over my senses. Each barefoot step I took on the glowing sand brought joy to my heart as the cries of seagulls pierced through the thundering surf. Being the first time I had gone alone to the beach with Dad, I knew this special day would be unforgettable. And unforgettable it was, but not for the sweet warmth and joy with which it started.

My loving father doted over me and filled my heart. A fantastic feeling poured in as I considered my father might love me enough to do this. He wanted time with just me. He gazed only at me. Even the tiny annoying sand fleas went unnoticed. Nothing could go wrong as we dug holes and built small mountains of dry sand. The towering sand castle, built one handful at a time, was nearly complete when Dad whispered: "Jannie. You, your mom, and your sister will soon drive to Minnesota to live."

A sudden hurricane appeared out of nowhere in my young, innocent mind. This scenario could mean only one thing. My heart stopped beating, and a heavy void filled my chest, making it hard to breathe. I realized my parents might no longer live together, just like other kids I knew. From the school playground, I had heard the stories of heartache and family struggles from my friends; it made me so sad to hear what they were going through in their homes. Would this broken-hearted life soon become mine?

After a moment—which felt like never-ending emotional waves—I put on a brave face and replied to Dad as calmly and maturely as a strong little girl might do. Staring down into the sand that I now pointlessly tried to mold into nothing, I asked the most terrifying question to confirm my greatest fear.

"Are you and Mom getting a divorce?"

An uncontrollable flood of tears broke through my tense body at his reply, and I became limp. My day began like one walking carefree by the ocean in the wet sand, surrounded by familiar footprints. Each impression's size, depth, and stride told a story of who had stepped there. Suddenly, the last thin, bubbly wash of a wave sliced past my sand-speckled feet and up the gentle slope of the shore as if to snatch away an unaware prey. I watched as, within seconds, all of the beloved footprints were gone, and my feet slowly sank into the sand as the wave quietly slithered away. I now found myself lost and alone. My entire universe was only me on an empty, smooth beach with my half-sunken feet slowly disappearing.

How children respond to such events can change the course of their lives. When you find yourself on a small boat and appear to be all alone, you assume you must take the helm, even without the skills or strength needed. When tremendous unavoidable storms swallow you whole in the middle of a vast ocean, you struggle for control–driven by fear.

That is exactly what I did. Helpless to reason with or see beyond the powerful and uncaring storm currents, defenses rose in me to control my situation by desperately seeking approval and passionately pleasing everyone—all while drowning in a sea of low self-worth. The warmth of the comforting sand beneath my feet drifted away as the bites of the annoying sand fleas shocked me into the new reality of my situation. I suddenly saw myself snatched up and dropped onto the slippery, hard, wet planks of a small boat and shoved into the violent ocean. Nothing appeared familiar anymore. Fear gripped me as I gripped the wheel.

My life has been a journey that must be like countless others, but through all the highs and lows, I have discovered a soothing peace and lasting joy. My hope for you is to join me here.

Everyone feels pain. Everyone goes through experiences in life that we don't expect, want, or understand. Some of us come through to see the other side—circumstances changed, back on the warm beach. But many of us get anchored in the problems of pain, suffering, confusion, and anger. But there is hope: by illustrating the meaning and purpose of my pain and suffering while at sea, I want you to be able to see this hope on your horizon, the shore to head towards, and the time-tested path to follow. I did not pioneer this course or navigate it alone; I uncovered a well-known secret that has brought healing and strength through my challenges, weakness, and sickness.

You may find yourself lost at sea, grabbing tight to the helm as you pass over the white-capped waves of life, desperately trying to stop or evade the storm all around you. If this is you, then this book is an invitation. Join me on my journey, and I will help you navigate toward a restful shore of healing and peace.

The Brewing Storm

The long drive from Florida to Minnesota was unbearable for me. I stared out the window, watching scenes of normality flash before my eyes. A barn. A field. A family…still with a father. Holding each image from the window and recent memories in my mind, I tried to make sense of everything happening to me. Occasionally, changes from bright sunlight to shadows flashed my emotionless reflection on the glass. Putting together bits and pieces of arguments Mom and Dad had with one another, the only conclusion to draw was that the divorce was entirely my fault. They sometimes argued over my education and the best options for me. Therefore, I ruined their marriage. I somehow caused the erasing wave; I made every anchoring footprint around me disappear. It was my fault.

The crushing guilt elicited the only correct response I could surmise: I needed to fix it. It was my job. Therefore, I had to be perfect. I made people unhappy; now, I must please everyone. A better life was up to me. Nobody else could solve the problems of my world. Grabbing tighter to the ship's wheel was the only way to control my destiny and harness the terror seeping into my soul. My intense thoughts focused on keeping the fragile vessel from sinking in the violent sea.

Arriving in Minnesota was bitter-sweet; I could spend more time with relatives, but it was very far from the beach where I left Dad. Grandparents, aunt, uncle, and cousins were all much closer now. Even with the unfamiliar family, the voice inside reminded me I must now please all of them. "Be perfect. Make them happy with you," said the voice, "or more bad things will happen all around."

This played out in ways that my mom and dad could not always understand. I recall taking a trip with my sister to visit Dad. While I remember very little from my time, a wave of perfectionism suddenly burst through when it was time to leave. Mom had packed our suitcase perfectly before we left. Shirts and pants laid squarely folded and evenly stacked. Shoes somehow tucked neatly into the corners. Socks rolled tightly into themselves in perfect little balls. A flap separated the two sides purposefully. It looked flawless when we arrived for our visit. As I opened it for the first time upon arrival, the perfection brought a smile to my face: this intricate order and efficiency, laid out before me, momentarily dissolved the chaos of the rocking boat.

But when it was time to leave and return home, the packing was up to me. Try as I may, something was wrong with each piece of clothing, shoe, and item I set in the suitcase. It didn't fit in the steamer trunk. The folds in the shirts appeared obviously misaligned, while the stacks looked uneven. Shoes bent uncomfortably as I crammed them into the corners. How do you make a little ball from two flat socks? How did Mom put everything in here?

I can't be wrong.

I must be perfect.

Hold the course.

The suitcase's contents were a complete disaster to me. The mist of a bow-breaching wave blew into my face. The joy of my visit with Dad came to a crashing end as my boat crested over an enormous wave and fell to the trough far below. I didn't know when I would see him next, and perhaps this fault could mean never again. It was all beyond my control and abilities. Spinning the steering wheel to the left or right made no difference. Breaking down in tears and slowly losing my grip, I became inconsolable and collapsed on the deck.

Dad didn't understand why this was such a big deal. Try as he might comfort me, I still believed my inability to precisely stow items in a suitcase would end in significant harm to someone—maybe me. If I got home and Mom popped open the luggage, would I disappoint her? My confused little mind thought this could be just enough to cause us to once again move away from loved ones. My inabilities and failures were all to blame.

At some point, Dad helped pack my bag and convinced me it would be OK, But I did not forget this failure. My navigation map had failed me and my little boat, and I needed to do better in order to reach any peaceful shore. *I'm not perfect enough.* Deep down inside, I wondered, am I simply not worthy of the beach? What bad things might fall upon my family because of my failure?

Staring out the plane's window while flying home, fears of imperfection tripped over each other in my head. The ground far below looked so peaceful and routine. Gentle wisps of clouds stretched as far as I could see into a soft, sunlit blanket. Green, brown, and blue patches melted into one another artistically in the landscape below—the mountains gently cradled the farmlands. I was a spectator to perfection and peace down below while a beholder of mess and chaos within.

Back at home, Grandma and Grandpa were the most loving, gentle, and caring people I knew. They were still married and gave me a taste of what a good relationship could look like. Sheltered from turbulence in their home, I spent memorable afternoons and evenings sitting with Grandpa and watching our favorite sports teams on TV. Grandma, in her doily apron, was like a ballerina in the kitchen, flowing back and forth in flawlessly timed movements, producing a magazine-cover spread for the dinner table. They had great joy, peace, and abundant love to share with me.

Time in their quaint old home was like a healing salve gently rubbing into my torn heart. While watching sports games, Grandpa continuously explained what was going on with each play. He showed me he deeply cared. I loved to learn the positions, how the scoring worked, and what caused the penalties. My efforts to learn made Grandpa so very proud of me. I could do something right and make someone happy with me. These precious, fleeting moments gave me hope.

My whole family went to church. While nobody in our family was perfect, they appeared to pursue God and desired to do better. As a child, the stories I heard, the lessons I learned, and the character of God became more and more real to me. It is hard to describe how you can see and believe something so firmly at that age. Perhaps in the same way you accept that air is what you breathe and the sky above is blue, I sensed God's presence and comfort when I thought about Him. My feeble prayers brought peace. When I learned Jesus calmed the storm while on a small boat at sea, I desperately wished that for my own tumultuous voyage.

I knew in my heart that God was and is real. Now, the challenge was to reconcile the experience of my world with the one described to me through the Bible. In Sunday school classes, I would hear verses of beautiful promises for how well life could go for me. Each one resonated in my emptiness. The overarching idea that God wanted the best life for me is what any child expects and longs to hear from their father. I hungered for those promises but couldn't grasp how to reach them. Alone on my boat, winds raging, Jesus asleep on the bow—I wondered if I would ever escape.

Unrelenting Storm

Dad moved from Florida to the Chicago area to be close to his family. A short time later, Dad married again. My new stepmother was kind to my sister and me. During the first summer we spent with Dad and our new stepmom, she would often play with us in the pool. The refreshingly small waves and sunshine distracted me temporarily. Stepmom focused patiently on me as we baked together. Lots of laughter filled the home, and love was all around. Despite the hard transition, I got used to having two families. I just had to live two lives separated by deep waters.

Step-by-step baking instructions and measuring tools allowed my perfectionism a place at the table. Oh, how I loved to bake. I could create with my stepmom, and the joy of eating tasty treats was the icing on the cake. Excited anticipation and the smell of sugary treats overcame the harsh sea air as I crouched and stared into the dimly lit oven like a smudged porthole window.

Spending time with Dad is what every little girl dreams of, but as dreams sometimes do, darkness crept back with my inability to control the scene. My stepmother became pregnant, and the boat swayed back and forth even more. As their new children entered their family, the welcome mat at the front door disappeared. When I returned, the oven remained dark and cold. The previous laughter-filled pool sat quiet and still—like the calm before a storm. Time with my father became increasingly divided, and I could no longer control it. He faded away as if slowly decaying into the darkness of a nightmare. Once again, the unpredictable ocean depths surrounded me.

Days alone with Dad on the beach slipped through my small open fingers like a handful of dry sand. I could do nothing to stop it as unknown forces beyond my control pulled everything around me downward. Try as I might to bring back the status quo, my place in family #2 appeared to be that of an unwelcome guest rather than a most-favored daughter. Awkward silence at the dinner table ended with me sliding off the dining room chair and retreating into a lonely corner of a room.

A glimmer of light shone on the horizon as another special day with Dad took form during one of my visits. We planned to go to the mall for a date, and this time would be better than the beach day, I imagined. Excited for the opportunity, my prettiest outfit adorned me that day. I washed the sea-salt spray off my face to reveal my porcelain skin. Tiptoed on the bathroom footstool, I brushed my thick dark hair in the mirror, practiced my happiest smile, and imagined my father lovingly staring back at me: the apple of his eye, the focus of his attention. What a perfect day this would be!

However, leaving my stepsister and stepbrother behind from a bonding activity was not appealing to my stepmother. As I brushed my hair in the bathroom, I could hear an uneasy tone with an increasing volume slithering down the hall from the kitchen. Few words were intelligible from behind my door, but the names of my stepsister and stepbrother squeezed through the cracks. Moments after the crescendo, Dad tapped gently on my door, opened it softly, and sheepishly confessed that our special event would now be less so for me. Stepbrother and stepsister would have to come along. No longer would I get to spend time alone with Dad. The side of his face became a more common view as I took my new place in the corner of his eye. Just when I thought my father might take hold of the helm to help me navigate the storm, I noticed the wheel drifting aimlessly back and forth—abandoned.

In church, I learned God would never leave me. Somehow, God's gaze upon me would never stop, and He guaranteed special times alone. God was the perfect answer and example of what I desperately sought—a strong and sturdy captain. The conflicting images between my father pulling away and God pulling me toward Him were challenging to resolve as a child. I already knew in my heart that the Bible was true and God was real, but how could God focus intensely on me while my father was so distant and distracted?

I resolved to hold tighter to the wheel on my own since no help came. The school presented a unique setting for me—one I felt I could control. The academic subjects and lessons all made sense with little effort. Schoolwork could be nearly perfect, and top grades became the norm. With a bit of pencil sharpening and only a few rubs from the eraser, my tests and homework made me and my mom proud. A powerful voice in my head convinced me that by working hard, I could please everyone, and through good grades, life would always be smooth sailing.

But despite my achievements, an eerie moan from the depths whispered of harsh seas ahead. As I slowly made friends at school, I came to realize I was the only one not living with a mom and dad at home. All of my other friends had both of their parents under one roof. With sturdy captains at their family's helms, many friends seemed shocked to learn this disturbing fact about me. Only I had experienced divorce, and this was because of my failure. I felt like I had drifted into their bay on a life-raft from a different country while they all steamed ahead in their yachts. I may as well have spoken a foreign language. A typical child would daydream about what they might become when they grew up; I dreamed, instead, about the alternate reality I desperately wanted to live in that day. If only the divorce had never happened.

The window to my dreams held the view of a happy little girl who could play and be carefree. Mom and Dad loved each other, and the family was intact. In that life, the happy little girl could be imperfect and her mistakes forgiven without harming others. Her actions had no effect on the world in which she lived. As I stared through this imaginary porthole window, my breath fogged up the view and reminded me of the cold, captainless reality where I found myself.

Leaks in the Boat

Sports and athletics were never my thing. Kids on the playground would laugh when I awkwardly missed the ball or fell while stumbling over my feet. I know this is common. Kids will be kids. Unfortunately, I believed I was the only one in the school who needed to improve. Swing as I might, I couldn't hit the ball. For a child who already felt that her imperfections had caused the crumbling of her world, this struck a raw nerve inside.

In some ways, you can imagine my partial relief when Mom announced we were moving again. The move was not as far as Florida to Minnesota. Still, the new home took us far enough away that I could start over at a new school with new friends and perhaps reinvent myself into the perfect girl I needed to be. *After we move, everyone will love me,* I imagined. The sky would always be blue. I had learned lots of lessons about what to say, how to act, how to look, and how to avoid embarrassment. Surveying my rocking lifeboat, rope entangled me with a web of fixes, knots, and control mechanisms from stern to bow and from port to starboard. Problems at school in the past could stay right there. My new, all-encompassing constraints would hold me on my feet and my boat on course.

The new town was small and very rural. I recall soaking in peaceful and perfect views from the dusty car window as we rolled into town. Are we finally moving to normality? A confident wave of inner strength carried me into the new school. "I can do this!" came the bold voice from deep within me. Lessons learned in the last school yard now felt like a lifetime ago. Fitting in shouldn't be a problem for a perfect new girl like me. Since this town was typical, maybe the kids would welcome me with open arms and bring me into the center of their friend groups. At the very least, I could avoid being alone, lost at sea. The welcoming joy of belonging flashed as a lighthouse above the school entrance on the first day.

The only problem with my one-step plan was that I came from somewhere else. Not only did I not grow up in that town or know anyone, I was not typical. My family was not like others. That minor detail escaped me. Perhaps I thought nobody would ever have to know my differences and what I had done to my family. If they discovered the truth, I would deserve their teasing scorn—the divorce was still my fault.

It did not take long for the other kids to see an unfamiliar face and realize I was not one of them. My embarrassing lack of farm knowledge and lingo hindered my friend-making hopes, and my farm-inappropriate outfits stood out like a red buoy in a sea of blue jeans. I publicly humiliated myself by mispronouncing some farm animal names and drew shame by never having thrown a cowpie like a frisbee. Knowing how to milk a cow determined if you were "in" or "out." I started outside and was never let in. I quickly learned that the school's lighthouse warned of danger ahead and not an invitation.

Classwork still came easy, and I could do better than most of my classmates. Of course, this doesn't help make friends when stepping into a precarious situation. Soon, I became lonelier than ever—the complete outsider in every way. I felt like my boat in the storm was now leaking through the cracks in the creaking planks. While trying to control the ship with one hand, I needed to plug the holes with the other hand. It was a stretch. Still no shore in sight. When will this ever end?

Mom started dating a man in this rural town and soon got married again. My second dad brought a large extended family spread around that town and local farms. Excitement grew in me as my first extended family gathering exceeded my limited imagination in sheer size and scope. Though unfamiliar, my new captain seemed to know what to do. Jumping out of the car and onto the farmyard into a crowd of children laughing and playing while aunts and uncles watched and talked, I could only imagine this would turn out well. Now, I am a part of the town and culture. I could step onto their boat and at least have safety in numbers. They will help me fit in and teach me to milk a cow. Standing on the edge of my boat, holding a rope with one hand, I stretched out my foot and readied myself for the leap onto this new, stable family vessel.

But their ship never quite came close enough for a leap. It was not the family's fault that they didn't know what to do with these city slickers. New to the town, new to the family, and only one pair of blue jeans between the three of us, we simply didn't fit—even from inside the family. The laughing and joyful kids all around me only played with each other and in games I didn't know. No hand stretched out from their deck railing, inviting me aboard. I felt like Rudolph, the red-nosed reindeer with an awkward flashing nose, telling them all to stay away and not invite me to their games.

Traveling back to visit Dad for the summers, I no longer fit there either. Once again, the waves had washed over my feet and erased the footprints in the sand. People and family were all around me, yet loneliness rose within me. Hungry to find acceptance in school and family, I strove harder and harder to do well, make everyone happy, and have a brave face.

After only a few hot and humid summers and finger-freezing winters, I must have done something wrong again. A summer spent with Dad and his family went as well as possible. My stepsister and stepbrother grew older, and their parents focused more on them. I'm sure that I wasn't a princess the whole time, but what had I done to bring back the dark skies? When I arrived home at the end of summer, Mom told me she and my new captain were getting a divorce—it must be my fault again.

The rocking of my boat would eventually become greater while pushing over many more breakers to another new town. When peering over the side into the bottomless ocean, fear gripped me. Now that fitting into the rural, ordinary town turned out to be impossible for me, could there be any hope anywhere? Next time, it will be different, but I realized my plans stink—like the rotting seaweed clinging to the cleats of my boat. With each hope of a fresh start and a new future, events would unfold to show I was not in control.

Throughout this time, the church was still a part of my life. Now, the promise of hope and a better future rang loudest from the tall, majestic church steeple. Giving up was never an option, but even standing outside the impressive brick building, I had the impression of being an outsider who was not welcome. With Jesus standing and calling me from the entrance, those inside seemed to have their backs turned. I knew God's heart for me, even if all others failed to show it. I had hope for a strong and steady captain in my life. This must have come from the Bible stories I learned and the presence of God I felt.

Taking on Water

Silly teenage years emerged. The new town contained two esteemed colleges. A more diverse population brought the potential that I could blend in easily. There was no more chewing on straw or milking of cows, and there were undoubtedly other kids steering their own boats. Anyone who remembers their teen years would not assume life got easier, and it didn't.

As the struggles of a young child trying to figure out the world slowly drifted away like a detached lifebuoy, the new challenges of social acceptance created a strong headwind to fight against. Most young girls experience social trauma at this point in their lives and would do what they could to avoid it. I went about it differently. I pursued drama—not socially, but on the theater stage.

The whole thought of escaping my reality and pretending to be a different person (a better person) had such deep personal appeal that much of my life soon focused on acting. Like the stage curtains pulling back in front of the actor to an applauding audience, I became happily surrounded by a group of accepting friends. Theater became my life. Directors would often cast me in prominent roles. The audience praised me from behind the bright stage lights. My dream world came to life on the elaborate stage with full-color lights. What better way to fight the battle of a storm than to pretend it does not exist?

During this time, my academics remained in focus. Getting "A" grades was possible while working jobs and memorizing lines for the theater stage. Still, the perfectionist voice inside of me insisted on excellence. The highest grades became the only option. The few times I fell short devastated me. A flood of emotions stirred up memories and fears that my failure (even getting a "B") could somehow ruin my smooth fantasy sailing. Like a superstitious belief, my lack of perfection could sink my boat.

Now that my social base had gathered to perform on stage, extracurricular activities shored up my self-worth. The French Horn became my way of demonstrating talent and skills I didn't possess on the baseball field. The speech team showed those around me I could think swiftly on my feet and publicly lifted my status in ways that a discrete grade on a paper could not. As a cheerleader, my classmates could all see me and adore me. I was back in control, even though I didn't know my heading.

The colored stage lights did not always shine brightly for each act. Cheerleading gave me additional friends, but I got an unexpected splash in the face one day. Another cheerleader made a simple passing remark that I might do better on the team if I lost a little weight. The comment was not just a simple splash. The water felt solid, like a tail slap from an escaping seal. While I was almost perfect with the things I did, my physical appearance left something to be desired. Compared to the other perfectly formed cheerleaders, I could see a difference in my bedroom's full-length mirror, which I tried my best to ignore. The imperfections, now spoken out loud, exposed the cracks in the mirror I thought only I could see.

Everything was going as well as it could until this moment. Now, I felt as if I was laying paralyzed and face-up, spread out and vulnerable on the wet sand of the ocean's edge. No strong and steady captain to help pull me to safety as waves rose up and then pounded down upon me, one after another. The thought of,

"Oh no! Not again!" would come as I held my breath for the next cresting wave. I could not run away from this. Solving the problem required a creative solution.

I had recently read a magazine article that might hold the answer. The article contained a lot of scary facts and statistics, but ultimately, I convinced myself that the pros outweighed the cons. Even though the factual statements from doctors were trying to warn and wave people away, bulimia seemed to be a perfect fit for me. At least, that was the way I saw it.

The eating disorder was not a disorder if I controlled it, right? Control is what I did best on my boat. Anorexia didn't appeal to me. I enjoy eating food as most people do. Bulimia provided the option to eat everything and anything with the promise of losing weight at the same time. Perfect! So long as I could throw up in time, food wouldn't hurt me. My body would become more attractive, and boys and other cheerleaders would approve of the change. That would solve my greatest problem. In addition, I would still be in control of everything.

For my remaining years at high school, this was my new tool for dealing with my uncomfortable genetics. Slowly, the tricks of the trade became clearer in how to hide the purge. I felt good. I looked good. I had ultimate control, and that, too, made me feel better. This time around, perhaps that wave would not crash down upon me. Like Moses parting the Red Sea, the wave would split before me and not touch me as I lay there on the sand—or at least so I thought.

After finishing high school near the top of my class, the storm of my childhood blew away. Socially, I was acceptable, which is easy for a people-pleaser to attain. Academically, I was excellent, which can build one's self-worth and scratch the perfectionist's itch. Musically, I could sing and play an instrument better than most of my peers. Through acting, I could escape and bring all of my success in life into my fake world.

On the surface, everything was perfect, as well as it must be. Lurking below the surface, more leaking cracks formed on the hull of my shrinking and sinking boat. Now, controlling my eating was controlling me. I could no longer sit down for a meal and enjoy the smells, colors, flavors, and textures of food. A carefree mealtime conversation at the table, laughing and joking about the day, fell upon my deaf ears with disgusting thoughts of what would come next. There always had to be a plan. Where would I eat next? Where could I get rid of it without a trace after the meal and before it was too late? Do the leaks in the boat even matter if, through nausea, I can bail it out fast enough?

I set course for college and a profession that could highlight my exceptional talents. In my sights was a career as a news broadcaster or a CIA spy. These careers could show my abilities, my perfection, and my high value. Once again, I moved far away from my troubles in the north and attended a university in Texas. Back then, living in the South meant that most students considered themselves Christians, but only a few of my friends actually attended church. Others would pretend they'd go.

The few times I attended a church worship service, everyone dressed to the nines and acted as perfectly as expected. The next day at college, with big, perfect hair with a bow, their wobbly sea-legs spoke louder and opposite as they lived and talked unbecomingly. After only a few visits, the church had become unappealing in that social setting. Now that I was on my own and away from home, I could make all the decisions. The double lives I saw in others also became my own.

Once again, verses from the Bible would come to mind about how much God cares and loves me, but was I worthy of His love? On the surface, yes, but what could God see, hidden from all others? The bow in my hair said I was beautiful and perfect, but I knew the darker ugly truth.

Four years of living a lie, from high school into college, caught up to me. A friend, who had more medical knowledge than me, figured out my mealtime spy game. She knew what it meant when I casually asked to excuse myself from the table shortly after a meal to use the bathroom. Returning to the table with a flushed face and red, watery eyes was not the perfect disguise and exposed my seasickness. In private, she approached me and suggested I at least get a health checkup to see if my electrolyte balance was off. Bulimia would cause lifelong damage to my body if I continued, and the perceived benefit would certainly not be worth it. This chemical imbalance could indicate that more harm was happening below deck.

It did not surprise the campus doctor to see a new patient, but a curious look appeared when I asked to have my electrolytes tested. Knowing that a confrontation was best for me, the doctor said, "That is an interesting test to request. Why do you think you need this test?" He knew full well why. The genuine test was if I would confess the truth.

People might think I was just fortunate in this case. For me, I saw God's care. This doctor had done his residency in an eating disorder unit. He knew the indicators and medical implications of bulimia all too well. He also understood he needed to gently and firmly insist I get help before it was too late. In essence, a professional was telling me to my face that my boat was slowly breaking apart. Nobody had ever said anything like that to me before that moment. Self-control was what I did best, or at least so I thought. I needed to regain mastery of that which now controlled me.

Everyone has decisions throughout their lives—some big, some small. Even among the significant choices, a few become our defining moments. When struggling through a mega storm, one might hold the course and hope that someday the clouds will miraculously dissipate and allow you to sail through life with blue skies and calm seas dead ahead. This unfounded hope can be the easiest to imagine and requires a negligible change in your actions. You must only grip the wheel tighter and try to head straight.

At this buoy point in my life, off to the right, the silhouette of land appeared far off in the distance through the wind-blown downpour. Do I change nothing, hold the course, and hope for the best, or do I head to the possible safety of a shore over there?

Wiping the drips from my brow and admitting to myself that I was no longer in control, I made what seemed to be a brave decision. I followed the directions of the doctor to see a campus psychologist and joined an eating disorder support group.

I'm not exactly sure why I did this. A still, small voice inside me grabbed the ship's wheel and firmly spun it clockwise while I stepped back in awe. With the wobble to my stance caused by an abruptly turning and tilting boat, I immediately headed in a new direction. I stood at the helm, but now, ahead of me, a blurry shadow brought hope of solid ground–an escape from the terrifying, lonely sea. Whether rocks or sand awaited me there, I had a new peace that someone helped guide me this way.

A New Course

As I boarded the plane to return home to Minnesota, a heavy feeling of failure consumed me. My messily packed bags weighed a ton and forced me to slouch over as I plodded through the airport terminal. Stuffing them in the overhead bin and under the seat in front of me, I curled up, being squished by the unpleasant truth. Once again, looking out the small window from cruising altitude, the slow passing of mountains and crop circles reminded me that everyday life was still out of my reach.

Mom had high hopes and high expectations for my education and career. She could see my academic achievements and believed in me as she bragged to others how far her daughter would fly one day. Though not always praised for the grades I brought home, I pleased her by not failing—until now.

My self-steering boat carried me closer to shore with safety now in my sights. Not giving up on myself, I chose a Christian counselor back home to get back on track. A job provided me an avenue to excel and prove my worth. The local gym became a distraction I could enjoy as much as any non-athlete might. While trying to regain control of my life, counseling proved most beneficial.

My counselor showed kindness, gentleness, and understanding. She seemed to know my secrets, my thoughts, my hurt, and my pain before I even spoke them. She treated me like a starfish, washed up on shore and tangled in a fishing line. One by one, she carefully took each loop off, knowing the solution to the knots. Then, the session came when she was ready to throw me back into the water. She stopped me in mid-sentence and offered, "Jan, do you realize you are telling God that you don't like the way He made you?"

Like a rogue wave unexpectedly crashing over the bow, the overwhelming thought knocked me off my feet and swept me to the rear of the boat. Tears unlocked floodgates, holding back years of hurt, guilt, and pain. Soaked in my tears, I don't recall if I had ever admitted or confessed anything like this to God. Oddly enough, instead of the water filling the boat, my salty tears lightened the load as I now rode higher above the waves with this release.

I read Psalm 139 over and over. These words lifted me above the oppressive storm to the overwhelming brightness of the sunlit side of clouds.

You have searched me, Lord,

and you know me.

You know when I sit and when I rise;

you perceive my thoughts from afar.

You discern my going out and my lying down;

you are familiar with all my ways.

Before a word is on my tongue,

you, Lord, know it completely.

You hem me in behind and before,

and you lay your hand upon me.

As I read these words, a powerful, personal image of a strong and steady captain entered my mind. New perfectly formed footprints surrounded me on my beach. Later in the same chapter, verses built upon that foundation.

Where can I go from your Spirit?

Where can I flee from your presence?

If I go up to the heavens, you are there;

    if I make my bed in the depths, you are there.

If I rise on the wings of the dawn,

    if I settle on the far side of the sea,

even there, your hand will guide me,

    your right hand will hold me fast.

If I say, "Surely the darkness will hide me

    and the light becomes night around me,"

even the darkness will not be dark to you;

    the night will shine like the day,

    for darkness is as light to you.

These life-giving truths echoed in my mind and heart all day as I went to work. While working out at the gym, I stared into my eyes through the floor-to-ceiling mirrors, and these truths pounded into my heart with each repetition of weights. Then, the verses in Psalms continued to a concept I had never fully understood or even read before:

For you created my inmost being;

    you knit me together in my mother's womb.

I praise you because I am fearfully and
wonderfully made;

your works are wonderful,

I know that full well.

My frame was not hidden from you

when I was made in the secret place,when I was
woven together in the depths of the earth.

Your eyes saw my unformed body;

all the days ordained for me were written in
your book

before one of them came to be.

How precious to me are your thoughts, God!

How vast is the sum of them!

Were I to count them,

they would outnumber the grains of sand—

when I awake, I am still with you.

God made ME! God knit me together precisely
how he planned from before conception. So touching,
encouraging, and uplifting were these words that I
had gained the courage to stand back up and regain
my footing after only three months.

The skies, again, cleared. From the helm of my boat, I could finally see the thin strip of beach ahead of me as narrow streams of sunlight poked through the gray. I desperately wanted to be there, and a comforting wind to my back pushed me with a gentle strength. The direction my captain now pointed seemed obviously best.

Realizing that my last college experience would be unwise to reenter, I sought a true Christian-based college. I needed a better place to sink my feet. Fortunately, I knew of one. My grandfather had been a professor at Wheaton College in Illinois. My mother and father had met there. Even though their marriage did not end well, I knew their problems were not because of God or the wisdom in the Bible or the college. The soft, warm beach ahead grew closer by the day. I had nearly forgotten the feeling of sand between the toes.

Solid Ground

I visited Wheaton College when I was in High School. With only a couple thousand students, the college seemed too small for me back then. I had bigger dreams and lofty goals in life during high school. At this point, I just wanted off the water. The boat had been my life for too long—there never seemed to be an end to the tossing and turning. I sought the stability of the shore, and now, realizing God had become my strong and steady captain, I felt more peace in the small college. It was as if God was about to pull my boat high onto the beach, beyond the reach of the surf, where He was waiting for me.

The college accepted my application as a transfer student with barely enough time for me to figure out the details. I had peace under pressure, believing the boat's rocking would stop at any moment. As the gentle waves turned into an excited surf, just before reaching shore, everything sped up as the last wave thrust the boat onto the safe beach.

In most ways, the college environment was everything I had expected. Stepping out of the boat for the first time, surrounding me were other students from across the country and around the world. They not only talked about God and church, but their actions differed from my last experience. These new peers were passionately wanting to live out their lives for and with God. Most students joined school-sponsored, student-led ministries as their extracurricular activity instead of partying. On my first Sunday there, the dormitories cleared out as everyone headed to churches throughout the area.

The buildings on campus reminded me of churches as I walked to classes. Large brick and stone buildings showed God's strength all around me. Our campus chapel, bigger than any of my previous churches, was central to my new community and attended daily by all in the middle of our class schedules. No longer was God on the periphery or far up in the heavens. He became the primary focus and life purpose. My wobbly sea legs struggled to adjust to a whole new world, but as I staggered on this refreshing beach, I could see that everything built here was not on sinking sand.

After only a week or two, a young man came into my life. Our dormitories connected in the middle by a locked door and occasionally opened to allow access for a few evening hours for young men and women to safely mingle. I wandered onto the boys' side of the beach to meet new classmates and stumbled into a mood-lit, plant-filled hut where a handsome young man sat alone listening to cool music. We instantly hit it off. I suppose there was a sparkle in both of our eyes at this "meet cute."

Greg had a confidence about him that was refreshing and attractive. His goal after he graduated was simple: to head to Japan and be a missionary to tell all about God's love. Wow! I had never met someone with such a strong passion for God. To this point, my friends only looked like Christians or attended church socially. Here was someone who wanted to live out his life as described in the Bible. Fortunately, Greg wanted to be with me as much as I wanted to be with him.

We immediately started having meals together in the dining commons, going on evening walks, and attending church together on Sundays. Greg spent time talking and praying with me. No friend had ever wanted to spend time just praying with me. Now, I could feel my cold, wet feet pushing deeper into the soft, dry, warm sand of joy, and God was right there with us.

Days turned into weeks, but only a few weeks passed before Greg and I started dating. With so much time spent together, the "M" word (marriage) stuttered from our lips only a month later. Some friends thought we were crazy to talk like that so soon, but Greg pursued me with kind and gentle love, demonstrating to me he would always put me first and do what was best for me. He looked and acted like the captain I needed.

Sure enough, only a few months later, Greg proposed with a ring he designed and had custom-made especially for me–a one-of-a-kind. Accepting the ring and placing it on my finger confirmed that my future looked bright. A godly man wanted me and chose me. I felt God's love as the one who sent Greg to love me. This relationship confirmed it: God cared for me and wanted what was best for my future.

Greg was in his senior year and finishing his degree in psychology. With my break in college and the loss of some transfer credits, I still had more semesters to go. Not wanting to draw out our engagement, we married that very next summer, a short time after Greg graduated. My mother had always warned me not to get married before I turned 21 years old. So, being a people pleaser, I had my birthday on a Monday and got married the following Saturday. I couldn't wait any longer.

A trip to Greg's home allowed me to meet his entire family. His mother and father were still married. His brother and sister treated me like an original member of the family. This setting was the normal I had longed for my whole life and what I saw out the car window as a child. I soaked in the experience of being loved and accepted for simply who I was. No clouds visible. Up and down the shore, established beach houses confirmed I wanted to live there.

After our honeymoon, we moved back to Wheaton College so I could also finish my bachelor's degree. A small married-student housing apartment transformed into my palm-roofed tropical beach hut retreat. Greg got a construction job to provide for us because, of course, that is what you do with a psychology degree (he would often joke). It paid the bills. He learned the business, quickly developed new skills and ascended through the ranks.

My last classes at college were a blur. I lived two lives, but not in a bad way anymore. I had my school life during the day and my married life at night. Greg fully supported me in finishing my degree and provided a strong carpenter's presence without pressure. I finally plunged into a healthy church and Christian community. The beach life definitely agreed with me. I was so thankful that my strong and steady captain had led me to this place.

Getting married at a young age proved to be a good idea for us. Neither of us had lived independently or developed strong opinions on how to do things. As we tied the knot, we slowly learned how to tie even more nautical knots together. We adapted, adjusted, and figured out how to give and take. An important lesson that Greg had learned before getting married and living out: "A happy husband only comes through a happy wife." With that mantra in mind, my carpenter often said, "Whatever you want, Jan." I chose where we would eat on date night. We would do what I wanted when I wanted. He also gave me complete control over when to have children and how many. He built our beach home with the rooms and furniture I desired.

The eating disorder that had plagued me for years was mostly gone. Control was still essential in my mind, but I could trust my young, strong master builder and our safe beach. Gone were the days of making plans to interrupt every meal, but the idea was not wholly foreign. After a few years of marriage, I decided to have a child. Of course, Greg agreed.

In choosing to have a child, one often becomes pregnant. With pregnancy comes weight gain. Physical changes brought back old thoughts, fears, unkind words, and the insidious draw to return to my old ways. Having no desire to return to the undulating sea, I asked my doctor and husband to help me stay on track. When those thoughts would come rushing back, I knew there was support around me and eyes closely watching. It was a difficult time, but I eventually grew to enjoy being pregnant. That birthed the love of being a mother.

Our firstborn, Matthew, arrived in the coldest winter month with a full head of dark hair. At church, we were part of a sizeable young-married class with couples having babies nearly every month. The support and encouragement we gave and received to one another looked like a utopian school of fish–swimming in perfect harmony. Moms could share lessons they learned and helpful tricks. I needed this tropical village, as only 18 months later, I had my second child, Natalie.

Greg and I served in the church, helping with the youth group and teaching in children's Sunday school. Church was not just on Sundays. It was now an integral part of my life. The more I pressed in, the better it felt, and the closer to God I grew. With two little babies to care for and a strong foundation, a cool breeze soon bled through the bamboo hut walls. The winds of change were coming.

An opportunity dropped in our laps for Greg to start his own business. We prayed about it and decided God wanted us to go. So, we sold our tiny house in Wheaton, Illinois, and moved over an hour north into Wisconsin so Greg could start designing and building custom homes with a land developer partner from our Sunday school class. Our new beach hut sat only a short distance down the beach from where my boat had landed, but the trek through the thick sand proved too far for regular visits from the villagers I grew to love. With my fearless husband by my side, even this kind of venture had become possible and not terrifying.

Our new abode, an old farmhouse, sat alone on land that Greg and his partner planned to develop. While the house had far more space and rooms than we had left in Wheaton, it was still an old farmhouse. The water-stained hardwood floors creaked, and curtains waved in a slight breeze from completely closed windows. Every creepy-crawly critter in our county sought refuge in our abode throughout every season. I was a young mother with two small kids, and all of my friends were now too far from our isolated hut for regular visits. At this point, I realized my need for a village, as only loneliness could be seen out every window.

The church experience in Wheaton showed me the value of being connected to those kinds of friends. We visited a few churches around our new area until we found a small, quaint church. On the drive home from church each Sunday, Greg would ask me if I had met anyone I would like to know better. He sensed my isolation and could easily see the solution. I had the ability to change my circumstances. So, Greg nudged me every morning before heading to work, saying,

"Who will you call today and ask to meet?"

Call after call. A village grew around me in those years. Soon, huts surrounded me on the beach that I could easily pop over and visit at a moment's notice. As relationships grew and our involvement in the church deepened, I realized I had lost control over where I lived, but it was OK this time. I didn't choose the farmhouse, but soon, we were living in a beautiful model home Greg had built. I didn't plan to move away from my friends in Wheaton, but God opened the doors of a welcoming new church, and now my friend circle had expanded. Greg started a business I did not foresee, but his success provided more than we could ever ask for by that stage in life. Slowly, I could release my grip on the beached boat's rope. The vessel I once desperately tried to control no longer decided my destiny, and it was good. I slowly learned to let go of control and invite God to order my steps forward.

A Rogue Wave

Surrounded by success in business, friends from church, and the comfort of a brand-new and impressive home, we had our third child, Heidi. I loved being pregnant, and Greg agreed to as many children as I desired, but I got what I wanted at this point. With these three children under the age of four and a spacious hut, I believed that life couldn't get any better. In only a few years, we ended up a short distance from my original beach landing to now living in what seemed to be a Malibu beach mansion. Nothing could go wrong now.

I don't know if the undesirable happens because things are going so well or if trouble comes whenever it wants, but shortly after coming home from the hospital with our third child, something went awry. Holes appeared in our thatch roof. I felt fine, but my muscle control was off. One day, I went to pick up a glass from the kitchen counter to take a drink, and the glass simply slipped through my fingers and broke on the counter. With a confused look on my face, I studied my hand in the sunlight coming through the sink window. What caused this? There was no oil or grease or dish soap. They were dry. The glass was dry on the outside as well. I tried again with other items but couldn't hold on to them. Not good. The holes in the roof would certainly let the elements in and ruin everything.

A trip to the hospital and several tests seemed to imply that I had had a stroke. Other tests revealed a rare and confusing blood condition. Something unfixable broke inside me, and there were no patches to keep the rain out. The doctor put me on steroids, which caused my face to become puffy. I called it my "moon face". Looking in the mirror as I brushed my moon-face hair, old thoughts and struggles from childhood flooded back. Patches of thatch from the roof fell down around me, but now my actions and decisions affected my entire family, not just me. I could not let this take everyone down.

Greg supported and cared for me as any woman would desire from their husband. He still told me I was beautiful and lent his strength to me. More and more houses were going up through Greg's booming business. Once again, we poured ourselves into the church, led youth groups, and helped run the services with me singing and my carpenter hammering the soundboard. As a married couple, events impacting one of us affect us both. The next wave had Greg's name on it.

Unexpectedly, Greg received news that his great-aunt, Jeanie, had passed away. She was a powerful woman but with the most petite and frail structure. Greg recalled as a child, whenever they met, she would come over and whisper in his ear during a gentle hug, "Remember, Deary, I'm praying for you every day." Something was different about her; Greg needed to fly back home for her memorial service.

While sitting in a pew surrounded by so many unfamiliar faces, Greg listened intently to the eulogy. The pastor recounted how she had taught their church's first-grade Sunday school for over 50 years until she passed. Nursing in the hospital during the 1960s, administrators rebuked her for taking her Bible on rounds as she read and prayed with patients. Of course, Aunt Jeanie ignored those instructions and continued to share the Good News anyway. The recounting of her meaningful life brought tears to Greg's eyes as he reflected on his original college ambition. Did he still have enough meaning and purpose? What the pastor said next opened his eyes and his heart more widely.

The pastor held up an old, heavily used Bible for everyone to see. He announced this was her Bible, given to him a short time before the service. As the pastor glanced through the worn pages, he saw countless marked verses with handwritten notes in the margins. Turning more pages, one after another, they had countless notes. He slowed down enough to read these notes and became overwhelmed to realize the notes appeared to be names. Looking more eagerly now, he deciphered her handwriting enough to recognize some names.

From the front, the pastor asked if he could read some of these names out loud for everyone. As he did so, strangers in the crowd raised their hands or stood up. One by one, the large group who gathered to pay their respects showed they were also in her first-grade Sunday school over the past 50 years. The pastor then raised his hand and confessed he had also been in her class as a child. At this point, Greg's father leaned over and whispered, "she led me to Christ when I was a little boy as well." She showed God's love to so many. She led them to Christ. She wrote their names in her Bible and continued to pray for her "Dearies."

Greg had a legacy epiphany that day. Even though we were doing well and serving in the church, there might be even more. This time, as Greg sat in the plane flying back home, he looked out the window and saw the vision of a new future for us—one with more meaning, purpose, and a calling. The forest-covered mountains below presented an adventure to explore. What would people say in his eulogy? How many lives would he have impacted? He sensed God calling us to something greater.

Upon returning home, we talked about what Greg had experienced. He asked, "What if I close the business, sell everything, and follow where God will lead us?" If that isn't me losing control, I don't know what is—completely surrendering my wonderful beach, friends, and church to only head back out to sea. The thought both terrified and excited me. My carpenter asked to get back in the boat, but could I trust his blistered hands to steer?

Greg discovered an opportunity with a Christian camping ministry in far northern California. He flew out to visit the camp director, and we prayed about this together. We agreed God was leading us, and the boat would take us there. Greg closed down his company and sold all his tools, trucks and trailers, sail and power boats, snowmobiles, and our incredible Malibu beach hut. After packing a few remaining items in a small storage unit, we loaded up our minivan like the Beverly Hillbillies and drove west for several days, trusting that God would now lead us. With our whole family holding on to the sides of the boat, Greg got behind and pushed us off into the opposing surf. When the boat would point toward the sky as it climbed the mounting waves, we all felt the excitement of the journey—even with the drop moments later. There was a lot of peace and excitement in no longer defining our future. The sprinkles of waves on my face exhilarated me. I felt alive!

This new season in our lives became a time of refocusing. Having a business and being involved in church gave us some meaning, but our new calling promised even more. Greg recounted how, after the funeral, he thought he saw two futures for us while he gazed out the plane. The first was that he would build a large company and an empire, but the work and focus could destroy our marriage and family.

He would end up alone. The other future took us to where God would lead, and we could fully trust that His plans were better. It mattered not how much money we had or how big a house we call home. We chose God's way. We chose the boat over the beach.

Step Toward Surrender

In the ordinary world, it is not by choice people move down the socio-economic ladder. Sometimes, businesses and jobs fail, debt consumes freedom, or divorce destroys families. The result can be that people lose their beautiful homes and have to start over. Rarely do people willingly give up a big, beautiful six-bedroom, four-bath, new model home and choose to live in an old, decrepit, single-wide trailer. But we did exactly that.

We had such joy in surrendering what we held on to before. Releasing the material entrapments, we lived a life of simplicity and followed God. We had moved to a small rural community in far northern California, mainly containing ranches and farms. A single two-lane road went down the valley surrounded by nearly impassable mountains. In that isolated environment, everyone was your neighbor, and that feeling was wonderful. While there were still waves in the ocean, we wandered through tropical islands and enjoyed the view.

Two different Christian youth camps in that valley had docks for our boat. The old Dumpy Trailer was my favorite. Mice nests discovered just below the old stove's cover didn't completely freak me out. The small room addition built off the side of the trailer was awkwardly quaint. Though a tad cold in the winter, the wood stove made from a rusty steel barrel worked fine. The entire trailer could have fit inside our previous family room, but we didn't feel deprived. The boat freely swayed moored to the docks.

This newfound freedom did not always come easy. When you feel you are on top of the world, choosing to go to the bottom requires humbling experiences. In our case, we quickly realized that it was actually a good thing. A hard pill to swallow was when the youth group at our church did a canned food drive and brought the food to a needy family in the valley—our family. Just a year before, Greg was making more money than we had ever dreamed while living in a mansion. Because of our choice to follow God, we now received charity from high school kids while living in a soon-to-be condemned trailer. With big smiles on their faces, as they handed us many grocery bags of dry and canned foods, we smiled back and gulped, knowing humility swallows pride.

Greg served in the camps and had special projects, but those efforts paid little or no money. I served at the camp and soon grew into the position of assistant director, helping to run the camp and manage the summer staff. Our kids had friends to play with and obviously didn't care about their home's condition. We certainly struggled, but in the end, our marriage and family became even stronger going through these challenges. Sea legs grow strength by constantly attempting to balance on a rocking boat.

After a few years, we felt our time at the camp ending. It was time to leave this safe harbor and move on with our newfound humility. Greg quickly found a job a seven-hour drive south in Silicon Valley with a large housing developer. Starting the job before our family had moved, Greg found a privately owned rental home within the Mount Hermon Christian Conference Center near Santa Cruz, California.

This new home was a step up in so many ways from camp. The 60's themed color pallet of avocado appliances, shag carpet, and a mustard-yellow free-standing fireplace really didn't phase me. Still, a giant leap down from the picture-perfect beach we had left in Wisconsin, we found more contentment in what we had. At least our boat now had a roof to cover it.

My daughter, Natalie, told me she had been praying for a house in the woods with a balcony on the second floor, a spiral staircase, and a wrap-around deck. I thought that was sweet to dream about but never told Greg. When he finally brought the family down to the house that he had found on his own (without knowing Natalie's dream), I saw that the two-story house was surrounded by tall Redwood trees, had a balcony on the second floor, a wrap-around deck, and (for the first and only time in our lives) a spiral staircase prominently positioned, right in the middle. The waves we traversed added joy to the journey.

Even though we moved a seven-hour drive away from the Christian youth camp, our involvement continued. Greg stayed down to work in Silicon Valley while I took the kids up to live at camp every summer. These were wonderful years of fulfillment and plenty. I managed staff while the kids played all day around the camp. Greg moved from dot-com company management to a biotech IT project management consultant within a few years. We went from nothing back to abundance in the blink of an eye.

Our focus and involvement at church continued to be strong. Once again, leading Sunday school programs, singing in the services, and helping a pioneering offshoot of our church demonstrated our desire to serve God. From the bottom of the wave, life swept us up with the adrenaline rush of a surfer catching a great wave. We now rode confidently on the crest, having gone from rags to riches to rags to riches. Greg received monthly checks totaling more than our previous annual income.

We shifted from being the recipients of charity to helping the camp make it through its lean winter months. Our time of receiving charitable groceries turned into us covering the camp's payroll, buying whitewater river rafts and vehicles, and improving all of their office equipment and furniture. We had such joy in giving more than we ever had before. With the financial increase, we landed the boat on another beach and purchased another beautiful, spacious house in Santa Cruz, California. Could life get any better?

Tsunami

Life seemed so perfect. A few minutes' drive to the scenic cliff-backed beaches on the Pacific Ocean, our house was perched on a hillside within the redwood forest and looked out across a small valley over misty wooded mountains. Greg and I shared four cars. One was a cute, classic, red VW convertible that Greg surprised me with at Christmas. Successful new careers for Greg, life-giving engagement at church, and summers to remember at camp became our new pattern. These are the sunny skies everyone strives to live in forever.

Surfing the safe waves on our beach, Greg brought the whole family back up to camp again for summer and then drove back and forth to Silicon Valley. He spent days or weeks working seven hours away before returning to camp for the weekends to spend time with the family. Our perfect lives, living on an ideal beach, in a perfect house, were free from clouds. No sign of a storm on the horizon. No warning sirens. No lighthouse.

One day, while driving my kids to the store, I realized things weren't right. Suddenly, I saw two cars heading down the two-lane highway right at me. The center line was now split in two as well. In fact, everything in front of me appeared double. Needless to say, this was not ideal for driving. I had to close one eye, turn around, and head back to camp slowly and carefully.

I knew I had some sort of bizarre, rare blood condition that a local doctor monitored. Did this finally do something to me? This was not normal and didn't fit into our perfect world. My doctor insisted I immediately go to the hospital and get checked out. I knew I had wiped out on the wave, now churned by the wash with a mouth full of salty, sandy water.

My blood condition made little sense for the symptoms I experienced, so the doctors ordered additional tests. After the MRI, the doctor showed me the results and the lesions on my brain. A painful spinal tap confirmed the doctor's fears. I had MS, Multiple Sclerosis.

This news was no ordinary wave. This was a life-changing tidal wave! Popping up for air and looking around, everything I knew and trusted was now consumed by and swirling in the dark waters—all being dragged away. The house didn't matter anymore. Greg's income was meaningless. I had a terminal condition for which there was no cure, and the doctors said my life expectancy should be about 30 years. Later, another doctor reviewed my complete history and stated that my stroke, nearly a decade before, was probably the misdiagnosed onset of MS. How many years does this leave me?

The wave did not just wipe away footprints this time. Towering over me, the wave overcame my entire peaceful and joyful beach party. Nothing remained. I wondered how or why God would allow this to happen to me.

We served Him.

We surrendered our plans to His plans.

We left the beach and got back in the boat.

We gave to ministries and trusted Him.

Why would bad things happen to good people?

I'm a good person.

Treatment began immediately to help control the symptoms. None of the drugs could cure MS, but hopefully, they could slow down the progression. Three times a week, painful shots in the leg bled over into flu-like symptoms for a day. Now, I limped through life, not knowing the next steps or how long they would last. Doctor visits, blood draws, shots, double-vision, loss of taste, and sick feelings became the new norm.

Once again, I felt swept out to sea. I could see my house on the shore, but a riptide pulled me further away. Old thoughts, the days of struggling alone in a boat, crept back into my mind. I knew it was too good to be true. Normal could mean relentless storms. Once again, I had no control as the currents fought my desires.

One day, after Greg had left for work, I was reading the paper and glanced through the obituaries. An unfamiliar woman popped out of the pages. The notice detailed how she had died at 45 from complications of MS, and she had left behind a husband and three children. I completely lost it. Both angry and crying, I wondered how this could be possible after doctors promised I could live so much longer. Why, God? Why?

I had it out with God that morning. This cannot

be fair, and a loving God would never allow this to happen. Everyone I knew lived healthy and happy lives except me. What did I do to deserve this death sentence? I drove my kids to a friend's house that morning on my way to a regular appointment with my counselor. Doctors suggested I work with a counselor as so many MS patients struggle with depression. I was no different. When I arrived at the counselor's office, I was ready to unload.

As I entered her office, she saw my disposition and asked how I felt that morning. Obviously, not well. She then asked me if I had read the paper today. That was strange to ask, but I responded I had. She dug deeper to ask if I had also read the obituaries. She was getting a lot warmer because I had. My counselor then got to the point: had I read the one about the mother with MS? She saw it as well and had prayed for me and our time together that whole morning.

Talk about a bomb defuse. I came in prepared to explain all that God had wrongly done. The next moment, I realized God cared enough to lead my counselor to read the same thing and be prepared to help me walk through this. With only a few words, she snatched me up, floundering in the water, and got me back into a boat. I felt so humbled at that moment. God was not blind to my pain and suffering. He was not trying to torture me. In fact, He held my hand the whole time.

Days became more challenging. Greg worked hard to provide for us all and came home to do projects on the house. Church and camp continued with my regularly recurring shots and sickness. We settled into a routine we wished to end. Unfortunately, we had no solution or plan for how to get out of this. With me in the boat and the family in a wave-battered home, this could not last for long.

Back Into the Boat

When you ask God for change, you assume life to become better as He pulls the boat back safely to shore. We were still learning to trust God and listen to Him for direction. Looking back on our past leaps of faith, God had always worked them out for the better. It didn't mean it was always easy or fun, but we were in a better place when following Him. This increased our faith in what came next.

One spring, Greg had a funny sensation. He came home from work, sat down to read the paper in his chair as usual, and a sudden thought came to his mind, "Get ready for a change." This was an unfamiliar experience for him as the thought kept coming back at random times. What kind of change? How do you prepare for a change when you don't know what the change will be? Is this from God? The thought came again and again.

Eventually, Greg told me about this and asked what I thought about selling our gorgeous house he had been tirelessly working on and preparing for a change. Can I do that? Does the family really want to get back in the boat? Through prayer, we both believed that this could be God preparing us. So, we put our house on the market, sold it with little difficulty, and just in time to head back up to camp for the summer. Now free from a mortgage and no rope to shore, we were ready for a change.

So much uncertainty exists out at sea. What's so wrong with wanting to stay on the shore? The taste of salty ocean spray on the boat didn't compare to the ice tea in the sun lounge. Another storm could come at any moment. With my perfect life disrupted by the tsunami of MS, I relented to the boat.

Summer came, and summer went without a clear direction of what to do. Waiting on God proved to take longer than we expected. Throughout camp that summer, we looked around and listened, hoping to see God's finger pointing in a direction. With our bags packed and sitting in the boat, ready for a change, we simply drifted. No waves. No wind. No other shore in sight. At the end of summer, we returned to our hometown and found a house to rent, only one block from the one we just sold. Still ready to go. Often driving past the gorgeous home we had just sold, I wondered if we had made the right choice and were actually following God.

Greg became more and more restless with his career and was looking for change. Feeling a loss of purpose in earning lots of money for wealthy companies and helping them attain more, he came straight out and said that he desired to serve God more directly with his future work. With a merger starting between our summer camp up north and the Mount Hermon Conference Center, we wondered if there could be a place for us in the mix. It just so happened that we were involved in a weekly Bible study small group with the Mount Hermon director, CFO, board member, camp staff, and us. This seemed too much of a coincidence, and we can't remember how we even got into it. A change to Christian camping appealed to us greatly. We tried to paddle to that bay.

The church we were attending had a month-long mission conference that fall. Greg was traveling for work over the first two Sundays. Still, I heard amazing stories of how God led, provided, and miraculously took care of these missionaries. Earlier that year, Greg had read the book about the life of Reese Howell, *The Intercessor.* God had time and time again orchestrated

Reese's life into incredible encounters and blessings as he followed wherever God led and listened to His voice. While reading the book, Greg thought this could also be our lives. He imagined God at the helm.

On the third Sunday of the missions conference, a missionary shared his miraculous adventures with God. God perfectly orchestrated events and powerfully answered prayers. While sitting in the congregation, listening to the words and seeing the photos on the screen up front, I heard a voice say, "This is for you. You can do this."

At the end of the service, I turned to Greg and asked if he had heard that voice. He asked what I heard and suggested I go down immediately and talk with the missionary. Upon announcing our heart and skills, the missionary threw his hands up and shouted, "Hallelujah! That is just what we need now in our mission."

Our boat started moving by some force other than wind and waves and the wheel turned without a touch from Greg or me. I realized later that God's approach to this calling made incredible sense. Each of our previous significant life changes came through Greg responding to God. While I trusted God, I also needed to trust Greg through the change. At times, my frustration led to doubt and conflict. Finally, God pulled me first. I knew deep in my spirit that this calling came from God and not Greg.

We spent the next several months seeking wise counsel and advice. Were we crazy for leaving behind a profitable career and all the trapping of a wealthy life to go into missions? Some thought we were, and others encouraged us to follow God. Once again, selling almost all we had, we headed across the country with one car and a small U-Haul truck with what little remained. Like before, the sacrifice broke off the burdensome chains of our material possessions. Heading into the unknown became peaceful and exciting.

We drove from California to Colorado and recalled something from when we were first married. As a young childless couple, our first church together strongly supported missionaries throughout their hundred-year history. During one of those mission conferences, the speaker called for people to stand if they thought God was calling them to the mission field. Greg and I looked at each other, and with eyebrows raised and a slight grin, we knew what each other was thinking. We stood and responded to the call.

An exciting thing happened next. The speaker wanted those standing to commit to go WHEN God would call. Again, we glanced at each other and remained standing–committing to the promise. All these years later, the call had come, and we drove away from all we had accumulated to follow God.

The several-day drive across deserts and mountains seemed like a tropical tourist cruise between exotic islands. The new views around each bend filled us with anticipation for what new wonder we would see next. Finally arriving in Colorado, we walked into the old motel rented by a Youth With A Mission (YWAM) training location.

Our family occupied two adjoining motel rooms– quite a change from our previous expansive homes. Having been through something similar before, we knew how to do this. Living in the YWAM community looked very similar to being at camp. Instead of a dumpy trailer, we had old motel rooms. God had prepared us through our experiences to make this transition easier. Our new small boat, temporarily anchored at the reef of an atoll, felt safe knowing that a more exciting life would soon come. The shift that neither Greg nor I expected became much more personal next.

For the first three months of the Discipleship Training School, the requirement to serve in the YWAM mission, Greg and I sat through lectures each day. We both initially believed that our education from Wheaton would provide sufficient for our future missions. Besides, Greg had a Bible minor and studied Greek. I graduated with a Christian Education degree. What more could they teach us? This pride became exposed through these months.

Each week had a theme to the lectures, with speakers coming from all over the country to share their particular focus. One week hit me like an anchor on the foot. The title of the week says it all, "Surrendering Your Rights." Seeing that title in the syllabus seemed curious to me. I knew we had that covered as we had just sold or given away so many things we had gained. We surrendered all and could probably skip that week.

From the first day of that lecture to the last, I cried. Selling or donating things was much easier than offering yourself, your plans, and your control. While

I felt like I could gradually release my controlling nature, I trusted Greg to be my provider and in control. Greg stepped aside and said, "I am no longer the breadwinner for our family. I surrender my role as captain. God now is." Rather than looking to Greg, I needed to call upon God for my daily bread. Old feelings tried to sneak back, but new thoughts emerged, reminding me how God proved to be trustworthy.

Throughout the school, God continued as our strong and steady captain. As the lecture phase was ending, our class of 14 students prepared to hed to Thailand for two months. Just a week before leaving, two students still didn't have enough money. They tried all they could and came up short. The school staff sensed God wanted the students in our class to make up the difference. With time to pray about how much we should give, Greg and I split up and went in different directions to listen to God. As we returned to the classroom, I asked what amount Greg had heard from God. When he told me, I was just as surprised as he was. We had the same dollar amount. Within minutes, a very large check dropped from our hands into the offering basket. The total amount given by all students almost exactly matched the amount needed.

Greg confessed to me that our generosity would leave us broke upon returning from our two-month outreach overseas. We only had a little wiggle room left as we had already paid our entire school and outreach fees from our remaining savings. Trusting God is always fun, but it can also be scary as you throw your boat's provisions overboard while still far from shore.

Later that same morning, Greg received an email from a distant relative who stated that she had been praying for us and had an impression she needed to give us some money. You guessed it—the exact amount we had just given away hours earlier. Excitedly, Greg called an old friend to share the story of how God had given us back, within hours, the amount we had given away. Greg's friend interrupted and asked, "Was it this amount?" Confused, Greg thought he mistakenly already told his friend the story and amount, but he hadn't. His friend revealed how he felt earlier that morning he should give us that amount. God doubled our money given without asking.

A short time later, our whole family boarded a plane heading to Thailand, only 6 months after the 2004 "Christmas" Tsunami had devastated their country's shoreline. We traveled, with brand new passports, to the other side of the world to share Christ's love and help restore lives destroyed by a genuinely horrific wave. Such joy filled our family during these two muggy monsoon months. While I couldn't leave the air-conditioned rooms for long because of my MS, I could watch our leaders' baby and my children when the day's activity would have been too much for them. I was a part of the team, and the team returned daily with encouraging reports.

The view out the plane's window as we returned to the US was exhilarating this time. Traveling over vast oceans by air, our boat now had wings as we flew above the clouds. Despite leaving our safe beach and secure life, the unknown future became more confident as we trusted God. Our hope was now based on something real: God.

Losing My Sea Legs

Returning to our two small motel rooms, we had an important decision to make as a family now that our DTS school had ended. Should we join YWAM or not? We were still riding a high from the two-month adventure overseas. It would have been easy for us as parents to decide for our kids, but we knew that to continue further out to sea, our kids should also feel the call. If God wanted us, He would speak to our entire family.

We sat down as a family on our motel bed, and Greg shared with the kids the options. We could head back home to the beach house and restart our lives with all of their friends and familiar things, or we could stay with YWAM and see where God steers us next. With no emotion or prejudice shown for either alternative, we prayed for a few minutes and remained quiet to hear God's voice.

After praying, Greg and I both knew where God was leading, but Greg felt God wanted our children to answer first—we needed to trust God spoke to them. Refraining from giving our influential answers, we started with our youngest, our eight-year-old daughter, and asked what she believed God said to her. She confidently stated she thought God wanted us to stay in YWAM. With each child provided a fresh opportunity to share and disagree, each answer remained the same. Greg and I looked at each other with loving peace and knew our next step required us to pull anchor and set sail.

With no money left in the bank, we headed out to let all our family and friends know what God was doing in our lives—never asking for money as we felt God wanted us to trust Him for all finances. After a month of simply providing a map of our future to others, we settled back into our two small motel rooms at YWAM and served in missions.

Month after month, random people sent in random amounts. Our bills appeared to pay themselves, and we did not starve. God showed his faithfulness and ability to provide for all our needs. Even as the YWAM training base moved locations during that season, each step amounted to another simple wave. It was simply the rocking that one might feel on the calm ocean. No leaks or storms to contend with anymore. I didn't need to stand at the helm or try to grab the wheel. Our strong and steady captain maintained control.

Only 18 months later, it was time to set a new course. We responded to a ministry call from South Africa. With minimal planning and two duffle bags for each family member, we boarded the plane to fly across new oceans. Filled with anticipation and excitement, my sea legs felt different this time.

The type of Multiple Sclerosis I have is impossible to predict. I can go months or even years with no changes or effects. Other times, it seems like I'm falling down a flight of stairs to the dark deck below. We learned that heat and stress can bring on exacerbations. Heat, mostly, is avoidable. Stress, however, comes with life.

As we started the stressful transition from one continent to another, MS raised its ugly head and bit my legs. I became unstable and had additional difficulties walking. Again, the food flavors disappeared, and everything I ate tasted like metal. Pushed through the airport terminals in a wheelchair, MS shouted my weakness to everyone around, but in my ears most loudly.

In the past, events like this would be torrential rains, but unlike in the past, I had a growing trust in God. With each provision, each proof-positive, I knew it would be OK. Dealing with new limitations wasn't easy or fun, but I focused on God. Slowly, my walking cadence improved. Our family experienced a new far-off land and culture, but by the end of our time there, 18 months later, none of us really wanted to leave. But we knew from the start that God had called us for a short period, so we departed when our time was up.

After South Africa, we continued to allow God to steer. The supernaturally guided dart, thrown at the world map, landed on Montana. We had never been there before, but once again, trusting in God, we joined another ministry within YWAM. This new location put us close to their office in a spacious, lake-filled valley surrounded by snow-capped, forested mountains. One side of the valley was bordered by the Mission Mountains.

My balance never fully returned as I staggered on the boat deck like a drunken sailor. The stress of picking up and returning to the US shoved me down another step. Shortly after we landed in Montana, walking smoothly became a thing of the past. I dropped the keys to my car and picked up a colorful cane. Double vision, challenging muscle motor control, and confused perspective made driving dangerous—especially after 18 months of driving on the other side of the road in South Africa. This loss of ability took away more control and forced me into dependence upon others. Greg now did all the shopping, drove the kids to school and back, and did most of his work on a computer from home. I felt the ropes binding me to the side of the boat, unable to give a hand.

Even though I struggled with relying on others more and was embarrassed to have handicapped plates on our cars, my family and friends didn't love me any less. We knew God had called us to this place. Though the waves grew more imposing, we all took each other's hands in the rocking boat, still excited about what lay ahead.

Bumps From Below

Greg traveled overseas alone more and more for his mission work. He started special projects and taught in YWAM schools from India to Madagascar to Latvia to Bolivia—far enough away to know that he could not quickly come back home to help if I needed him. Each time he left, my kids provided relationships and community around me. A child or public transit could always drive me to the store or doctor when needed. Greg's absence was tolerable, with the rest of my family surrounding me, but the listing boat didn't feel quite right.

One by one, our children left the boat for college, over a five-hour drive away from home. The frequency of Greg's absence increased and drew out into more extended periods—sometimes up to five or six weeks. I discovered a unique spirit in Montana's people: independence. With independence comes a lack of need for others. The long winter months of ice, snow, and gray skies also meant fewer and fewer friends to see regularly. Stress slowly built up inside with new loneliness. I felt as though I was cautiously walking the plank off the side of the boat.

The day came when our youngest child left for school. The stress of seeing my last baby jump ship and realizing I now had an empty crow's nest added to the challenge of Greg traveling far away. Eerily, the boat seemed quiet and still in the ocean when a loud bump came from beneath, shaking the whole vessel. The gray winter skies of Montana vibrated through my bones.

I could not bear the isolation during the dark, frigid winters. Greg and I called upon friends to stay with me, or they passed me around to different homes while Greg traveled. This didn't solve the root problem. Friends still needed to leave for work. I considered myself a burden to everyone.

The increasing wave heights and strong winds beckoned the disturbing weather to come back. Old thoughts and memories trickled back into my shivering mind. Had God forgotten me? Did I not matter anymore?

Before Greg flew away on his trips overseas, I put on a brave face with a quivering lip and a fake smile. I told him I had everything under control and would be fine. Even with a few video calls in Greg's brief windows of opportunity, I curled up in my boat's dark, damp corner, trying to avoid the fear. After each trip, tears released on his shoulder joined the words from my lips, "I don't know if I can do this anymore."

Greg's separation increased my stress as I bounced around homes. I added to the work of others and piled guilt on myself. Greg helped many missionaries worldwide and knew God had more for him to do. "What about your wife?" came thoughts in my mind. Was God calling Greg to ignore me and my suffering? I couldn't control the situation. Am I not as worthy as those in need overseas? My husband abandoned me. My childhood came rushing back again as I desperately looked for any footprints left in the sand.

The situation frustrated us to no end. Full of fear, I walked to the end of the plank and felt like I would slip and fall as I struggled with my vision and balance. Greg knew God wasn't calling him to quit, but we couldn't see the way out. Gray skies and stormy weather enclosed us, even though we believed we were where God wanted us. Like the summer after we surrendered our house in California, we waited and prayed again for God's direction, now begging for Him to calm the raging seas as He appeared to be asleep during our time of need. We plodded forward, hoping something might change before we all drown. Perhaps Greg would stop traveling. Maybe I could become satisfied with being alone.

Trip after trip, month after month, we pushed forward. I sensed there were rocks ahead, and our boat may come to crash upon them at any moment. Here again, do we grab the wheel and make a course correction to what we thought best, or should we wait and follow God? We held tight—not controlling the steering wheel but wrapping the boat's ropes around our wrists as if bracing for impact on rocks.

One very average day, an email popped up in Greg's inbox. His father surprised him with the announcement that he just mailed a small inheritance check. Greg's grandfather had passed away several years before and left each grandchild a portion. As Greg read through the email and came to the dollar amount being sent, the picture of a camper, a trailer, or an RV popped into his head. The idea or concept hadn't been even a glancing thought for 20 years.

We knew that something was coming someday from his grandfather's will, but the exact amount stayed a mystery. Our initial plan consisted only of blueprints Greg designed for a single-room addition to our small house. This would make space for small groups and Bible studies to take place. Our little boat only needed a few enhancements in our minds. What did a camper have to do with that?

After finishing the email, Greg turned his attention to the room addition materials list. What could we afford, and what would we have to leave out? With each line item, Greg couldn't shake the image of an RV. The thought clouded his concentration until he finally stopped and asked God, "Is this from you?"

Listening to God, Greg sensed that our actual plan forward required him to surrender his travel, projects, and relationships overseas–everything he had built up over the years. He needed to open his hands and let the nails and tools slip through his grip. God's plan, coming at the last possible moment, turned Greg's focus toward supporting ministries worldwide while traveling in an RV with me. As soon as this complete concept entered Greg's mind, he agreed and saw the escape from our imminent shipwreck. God provided a life raft to save us with no time to lose. He calmed the seas.

Moments later, Greg approached me and explained the surprising revelation God had given him. He told me he would stop all of his travel and use his inheritance to provide a way for us to stay together all the time. I would not have to be alone anymore, which entered my mind like an explosion in the sky, parting the clouds and exposing the bright beams of hope. Greg would do this for me? God cared enough about me to provide us this way out. Wow!

We wasted no time looking for something we could afford. Old campers and trailers fit our budget, but once again, the excitement of following God made any option more than acceptable. Greg sent out an email to a few supporters and close family explaining that in the same way, each of them had believed in our ministry over these years and chosen to support us without being asked, we were going to use Greg's inheritance to invest in the future of our ministry. We requested no extra money from anyone.

Greg received several cheering emails and supportive comments. A few others didn't grasp the vision and left. Our choice of surrendering to God's plan again brought freedom, even if it meant living in the smallest quarters possible. Though just a life raft, it comfortably provided for our needs with a sense of security. We were at peace, even if we had to leave everything behind…again. As we scoured the web for used RV's, Greg's Aunt Rosie emailed. We didn't need confirmation, but God sent a dove with an olive branch.

Aunt Rosie had supported us faithfully over the years. A random amount would appear on our giving report each month, and she requested we use it for something fun. Throughout the years, her generosity had given us meals out, an ice cream on a hot day, and an occasional family fun day. This time, her immediate reply to our announcement was overwhelming. Scattered among the "Hallelujahs!" and "Praise God!" she wrote how she could see God's hand in answering our hearts' cries. In fact, she believed in it so much she wanted to double our inheritance. Also, more would be available for whatever equipment we needed in missions, as she said, "I've got your back while you drive down the roads." She insisted that we not just get an old camper but focus on "one of those large, bus-like motorhomes."

We went from tears and frustration to flying down to Palm Springs to purchase a class-A motorhome with everything one could need or want. We went from hopelessness in the face of rocks ahead to open highways in just one roll of a wave. Once again, like always, God proved His ways were better than our ways. He only asked us to follow. The hard part for us was to wait.

In hindsight, our times of surrender in the past made this transition so much easier. Going from beach to boat to beach, we could eventually adjust to this tiny raft, only big enough for two. Not knowing which road to drive down next week no longer added stress. Sheltered from the unpredictable weather outside, our home-on-wheels kept us together most all the time.

Sailing Into the Sunset

Over seven years have passed since we first got the motorhome, which we lovingly call Joy–the name given to it by Aunt Rosie. Traveling over most of Canada, the entire US, and even parts of Mexico, my friend-circle has grown exponentially. No longer left home alone, I now experience the sights and relationships the same as Greg as he continues to do his computer work while we travel. As soon as we arrive at a YWAM location, I jump out of the motorhome and volunteer in the community with the other missionaries.

Our home in Montana is now rented out full-time, providing additional support for our mission work. We continue to have what we need as God quickly replaces lost support with new people who feel led to give to us, all on their own. After 18 years, we always have enough and sometimes even more than enough. With our desires and needs reduced to the bare minimum, we've even surprised ourselves with how little we can live on these days.

Our kids have all moved to other locations. Still, with a motorhome, we can visit them more often and even spend extended time watching our grandkids grow. This, of course, is the hope and dream of any grandparent, and I get to live it now. The RV is a safe place for me to live with MS, and after more than two years full-time in our vehicle, I have peace.

In the Spring of 2023, both of Greg's parents passed away within weeks of each other. Shortly after that, Greg and I were driving back home from New Mexico to Montana and now looking more intensely at our sunset ahead. As we realized we'd now become the family's elders, we gazed into the most beautiful fiery sunset above the ocean with new dreams of our future.

This does not mean that I have completely overcome all of my feelings of insecurity and struggles with my values, but I have a new perspective. Recently, Greg wrote me an email of encouragement and perspective that helped sum up my life. I had never considered it this way, but life's arduous journey had a purpose. God was not torturing me for fun. He allowed me to go through much to shape me and mold me into who I am today.

In Greg's letter, he asked if I enjoyed where I am today. I had to answer that I was more satisfied and excited than ever. He then asked if I would prefer to be in a big house somewhere, filled with empty rooms, living the everyday life, or sitting back in our isolated house in long, dark Montana winters. I knew that neither of those options sounded better than sitting at my table just behind Greg in the motorhome. Lastly, he asked if it would be better to stay at home, sitting on our hands, and wait for the rare occasion of grandkids coming for a brief visit or instead live the apparent blessing of spending weeks and months with the little ones. If you are a grandparent, you know how clear and obvious the answer to that question was.

The emerald flash, as the last sliver of setting sun bounced off the ocean, caught my eye when Greg then pointed out that this was all because of me having MS. We would not have a motorhome if Greg's travels were not so stressful for me. Greg's traveling would not be as stressful if I could drive. The transition to a motorhome full-time could have been so much more stressful if we hadn't gone through the process of downsizing many times before. Letting go of things from inside our house would have been heartbreaking if we hadn't come through it again and again.

We are where we should be, even with MS or even because of MS. This leads to a promise in the Bible that I can now testify through my life experience:

> "And we know that in all things God works for the good of those who love him, who have been called according to his purpose." - Romans 8:28 (NIV)

So, my thoughts and prayers for all who may read my story are simple: Even as the pain of life sends you out into the storms, I know that trusting in the only One who can part the seas and calm the storms will be best. As I saw God as my strong and steady captain, where He led did not always seem good from where I stood at the time. He gave me rest on the beach when I couldn't last much longer. Then, He challenged me to surrender more and trust Him back in the boat. Each time, each boat, each beach formed me into the person I am today. Had I never left the shore, I can't imagine where I would be, but I know I am happier and more fulfilled today…even in a simple lifeboat.

Made in United States
Troutdale, OR
11/28/2024

25422192R00061